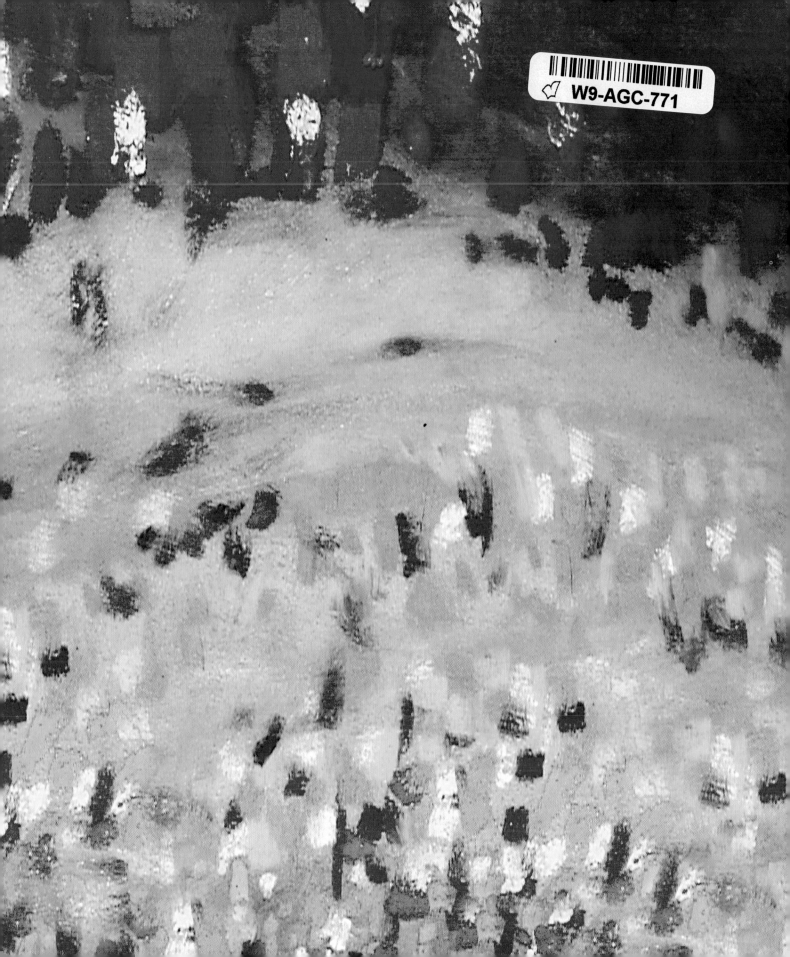

SEND ME *Tulips*

Kathe Oleson

Illustrations by Kristin Pluhacek

Send Me Tulips

Copyright ©2005 by Kathleen Brockman Oleson

Published by Prisma Press, Inc.

A division of Prisma Collaborative, Inc.

P.O. Box 650

Blair, Nebraska 68008

Toll Free 1-866-651-6123

www.prismapressinc.com

Text Copyright ©2005 Kathleen Brockman Oleson

Illustrations Copyright ©2005 Kristin Pluhacek

Design by The Sacco Group | www.thinksacco.com

Text set in Perpetua 14 Point

Printed on 100lb. Text Weight Matte Finish

Printed by Perfection Press, Inc.

Bindery by Pease Bindery, Inc.

First Printing 2005

Printed in the United States of America

ISBN 0-9702390-0-9

LCCN 2004115843

06 05 04 03 02 01

10 09 08 07 06 05

For those who read this book:

May each be surrounded in the light and love of Spirit.

May each walk their life path loving and honoring our oneness.

May each be enveloped with a knowing — some things in living

and loving transcend all human understanding.

May those who walk through the "Gardens of Life and Living"

know the transformational beauty of walking, running,

stumbling and occasionally being lifted along the path by Spirit and

through the love and friendship of Spirit's angels.

To Allyson, Eva, Retta, Tom and Megan —

In this life, may you know the alchemy created through love.

In loving remembrance

of

B. Gale Oleson

High on top a golden hill sat a farm with a stone home.
The home was surrounded by

...*trees*

...*flowers*

...*ponds*

...*fountains*

...*a waterfall.*

On the farm lived

…a man who loved life and living

…and a woman who knew love was the heart of life and living.

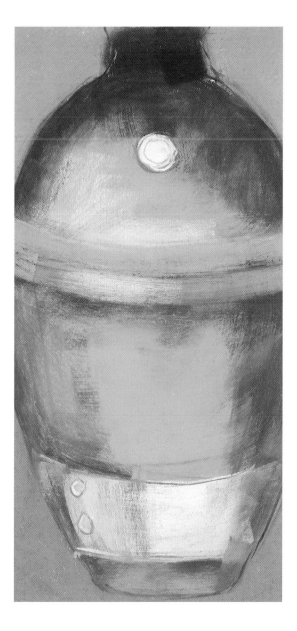

Through the years, the couple lived a full and busy life

    ...celebrating life events

        ...sharing the happy and sad times

            ...loving and laughing with family, neighbors and friends

                ...and learning through the challenges life presented.

Even when life-altering events occurred in their lives, they just seemed to adapt,

...*growing stronger as persons*

...*growing in their appreciation of each other*

...*growing bigger and brighter in their love of life.*

As the seasons passed, the man and woman

embraced this "time for being" as a gift to be treasured.

The man and woman could be found spending their days

…smelling the flowers they had planted

…watching the birds and butterflies come for visits

…listening to the waterfall

…eating the luscious, juicy tomatoes freshly harvested from the garden

…feeling the breeze as they took rides and walks around the farm

…talking with all of their menagerie: the ducks, the dog, the cats, the horses

...the fish

...embracing the love and laughter of the grandchildren, family, neighbors and friends.

As the couple breathed in the beauty of nature and the joys of life,

...*they reflected on the blessings in their life together,*

...*cherishing the memories past*

...*valuing the lessons learned*

...*delighting in the devoted friends and family*

...*appreciating the fullness of their life shared.*

In the gentle stillness of the evening, the man and woman each prayed for grace;

...each prayed they had been of service
and would continue to contribute lovingly and positively in the lives they touched.

The home on the golden hill seemed to glow

…in the light of peace and healing.

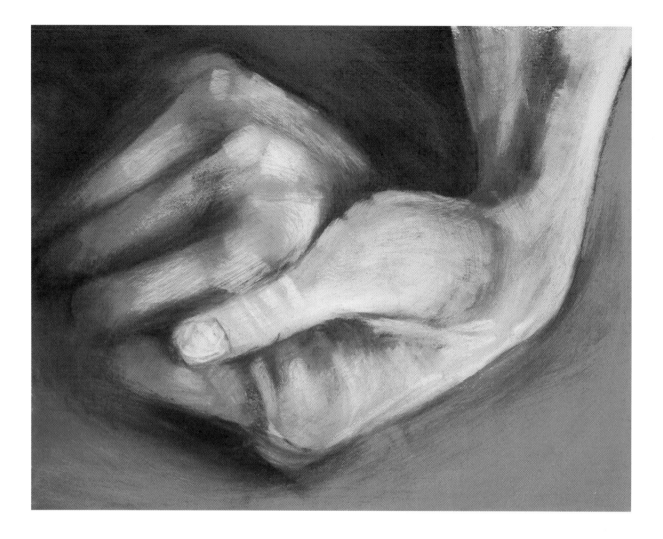

As the seasons passed, the couple realized they were going to be separated in time and space.

This made them very sad,

    ...longing for more

       ...more time

         ...more sharing of thoughts

           ...more creating of plans and dreams.

Through the sadness they celebrated the blessings in their lives,

...*the caring by all those surrounding them*

...*the love they held for each other*

...*the grace of knowing each was more whole for having
loved the other.*

In the quiet and reflective times they shared, the woman would speak of the comfort in knowing the man's spirit and energy would continue to be around her. She knew it would just take another dimension and form.

The man would ghaff at her comments, telling the woman he wasn't as convinced and didn't know how she could be so certain.

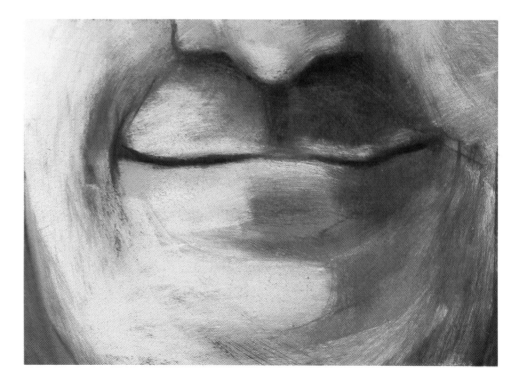

The woman would smile, her eyes glistening with unshed tears, while assuring him, "The 'next place' will be wonderful and beautiful and I know you will be so happy. You can send me a message, letting me know you are fine," the twinkle in her eyes saying, "and that I was right."

The man would smile his wide engaging smile and look at her skeptically. He would dryly comment, "Even if you are right, I doubt if I will be able to send you any messages."

The woman would smile back knowingly. She would remind him of what a determined and creative person he could be. Assuring him she knew it was going to be possible and that he would find a way.

He would proclaim, "I don't know," and she would smile and say, "You can always send me tulips."

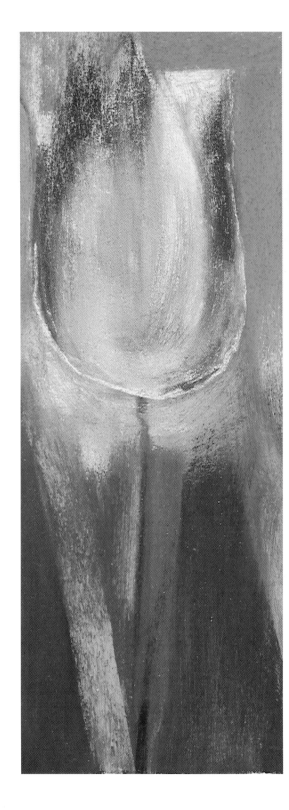

The days grew shorter and life on the golden hill grew quieter.

Friends, neighbors and family quietly came and went,

      …wanting to share the love they held for the man

            …with appreciation for his guidance, his teachings, his love and his wisdom

                …smiles and laughter would fill the room

                    …as they shared and reminisced with him.

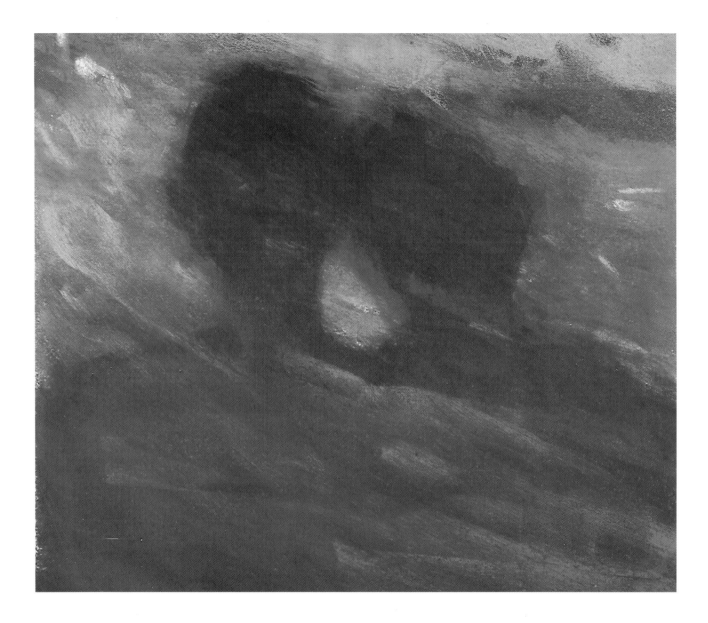

The couple quietly continued their conversations as they knew their love was all that was left.

And it was enough;

…the man would whisper "You are wonderful, you are my angel"

…and the woman would share how much she loved him

…telling him, "You are my hero filled with courage and strength."

The home on the golden hill became quiet;

    …the woman continued to share how loved the man was

        …what a difference he had made to so many

            …how missed he would be

                *…yet, she knew he was going to be so
happy and in such a beautiful place.*

Then one cold winter day,

…as the morning light dawned

…as the woman and man held hands

…the man smiled one last radiant smile

…and left the home on the golden hill.

The home on the hill became silent

…and the woman sat surrounded in the coldness and fog of grief.

In the following hours and days, though the woman was surrounded in the love and warmth of friends, neighbors and family; she was enveloped in a cold, numbing loneliness reaching deep into her heart.

She felt sad and alone

...drawing from deep within her

...grace and strength.

One evening, as family and friends were leaving, a special friend arrived to bring comfort and share in the grief of the woman. This young man…was especially treasured. He and the man had spent countless hours sharing the wisdom of the ages.

He held a bag in his arms

and quietly mumbled to the sad woman,

"I needed to bring something to you. I wasn't sure, but hope it's okay."

Quietly

   …he set the bag down.

The sad woman reached up and gave him a hug, sharing how pleased she was to see him.
She turned to the bag and opened it.

> *…As the bag fell away, a bouquet was revealed and she began to weep*

> *…first with sadness*

> *…and then with even greater joy*

> *…feeling a new-found warmth and comfort flood through her.*

Sitting before her was a bouquet of tulips

> *…twelve perfect orange and yellow striated tulips*

> *…and she knew*

> *…she knew in the darkness of that cold winter evening*

> *…she knew.*

Through her tears the woman quietly and graciously began,

…*"Thank you. Thank you for being his messenger."*

With her face radiating joy and her eyes twinkling through her tears, she continued,

"I told him he could always

...*send me tulips.*"

In the days and weeks to follow, the woman continued to be embraced in the
love of family, neighbors and friends;

...gently and slowly she began to feel the warmth and light of all the love surrounding her.

Though her life was different, the woman knew loving was the heart of life and living,

...and so she slowly moved forward, knowing life was a gift;

...it was about giving

...about loving

...about reaching out.

As the woman journeys throughout the seasons of her life,

…she continues to be reminded and comforted by the man

…each time he "sends her tulips."

And the home on the golden hill glows with love, light and laughter.

About the Author

Kathe Oleson, PhD

Kathe earned her BS from *Wartburg College* in Waverly, Iowa and her MS and PhD from the *University of Nebraska at Omaha*. Her extensive educational experience and personal spiritual journeys have formed her beliefs and view of our connections between this world and the next. A sought-after consultant and lecturer, she presents and moderates programs for mentoring, holistic development and caregiving. Through her consultancy, Prisma Collaborative, she facilitates the potential of individuals and organizations through the honoring of our oneness. Kathe spends her days in a peaceful, inspiring setting just beyond the verdant, rolling hills of Blair, Nebraska.

About the Illustrator

Kristin Pluhacek

A Nebraska native, Kristin is known for her use of vibrant color in interpretive pastel drawings. Her expressive spatial relationships and movement within the subject add a unique life to her drawings. Her works have been exhibited in fine arts galleries and museums throughout the Midwest, and are also found in numerous public and private collections. Currently, she lives a full life in Omaha, Nebraska with her husband and their two sons. She is an alumnus of *Creighton University*.